THE
QUEEN MOTHER

A LIFE IN PICTURES

THE QUEEN MOTHER

A LIFE IN PICTURES

With an introduction by
Michèle Brown

UNICORN HERITAGE plc

Copyright © Unicorn Heritage plc

First published in Great Britain in 1988
by Unicorn Heritage plc, Unicorn House,
White Lyon Court, Barbican, London EC2Y 8UH

Set in Century Old Style
Printed in Great Britain by
W.S. Cowell Limited, Ipswich, Suffolk

British Library Cataloguing in Publication Data

The Queen Mother: a life in pictures.
  1. Great Britain. Elizabeth, Queen, consort
  of George VI. King of Great Britain –
  Illustrations
  941.084'092'4

ISBN 1 870968 20 4

Design: Craig Dodd
General Editor: Michèle Brown
Editor: Mary Douglas

CONTENTS

The Royal Family

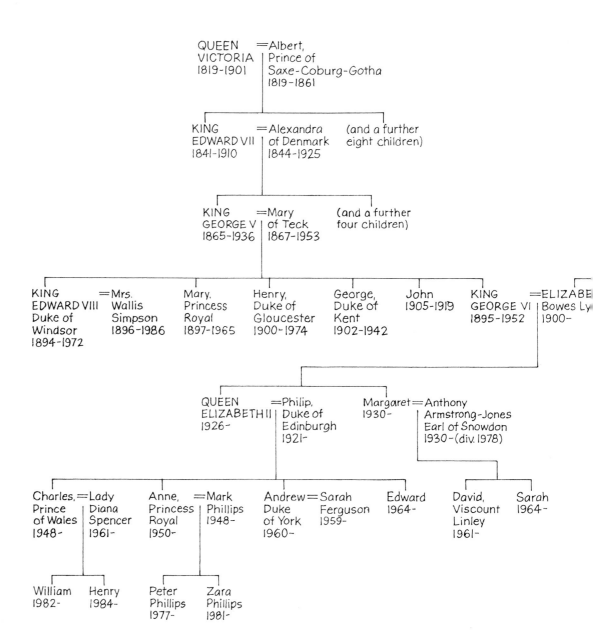

QUEEN VICTORIA 1819-1901 = Albert, Prince of Saxe-Coburg-Gotha 1819-1861

KING EDWARD VII 1841-1910 = Alexandra of Denmark 1844-1925 (and a further eight children)

KING GEORGE V 1865-1936 = Mary of Teck 1867-1953 (and a further four children)

KING EDWARD VIII Duke of Windsor 1894-1972 = Mrs. Wallis Simpson 1896-1986 | Mary, Princess Royal 1897-1965 | Henry, Duke of Gloucester 1900-1974 | George, Duke of Kent 1902-1942 | John 1905-1919 | KING GEORGE VI 1895-1952 = ELIZABE Bowes Ly 1900-

QUEEN ELIZABETH II 1926- = Philip, Duke of Edinburgh 1921- | Margaret 1930- = Anthony Armstrong-Jones Earl of Snowdon 1930- (div. 1978)

Charles, Prince of Wales 1948- = Lady Diana Spencer 1961- | Anne, Princess Royal 1950- = Mark Phillips 1948- | Andrew Duke of York 1960- = Sarah Ferguson 1959- | Edward 1964- | David, Viscount Linley 1961- | Sarah 1964-

William 1982- | Henry 1984- | Peter Phillips 1977- | Zara Phillips 1981-

The Earls of Strathmore

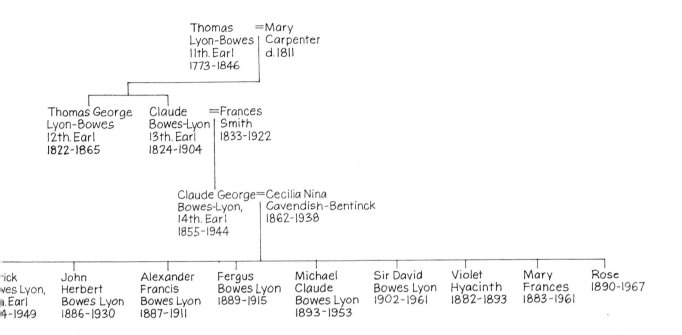

Thomas Lyon-Bowes
11th. Earl
1773-1846
= Mary Carpenter
d. 1811

Thomas George Lyon-Bowes
12th. Earl
1822-1865

Claude Bowes-Lyon
13th. Earl
1824-1904
= Frances Smith
1833-1922

Claude George Bowes-Lyon,
14th. Earl
1855-1944
= Cecilia Nina Cavendish-Bentinck
1862-1938

...rick ...ves Lyon, ...Earl 4-1949

John Herbert Bowes Lyon 1886-1930

Alexander Francis Bowes Lyon 1887-1911

Fergus Bowes Lyon 1889-1915

Michael Claude Bowes Lyon 1893-1953

Sir David Bowes Lyon 1902-1961

Violet Hyacinth 1882-1893

Mary Frances 1883-1961

Rose 1890-1967

The Queen Mother's Family Tree

Introduction

Enchanting, charming, fun, radiant, inspiring – words which recur time and time again when anything is written about the Queen Mother.

Nowadays, encouraged by some sections of the media, we have come to accept that behind flattering descriptions like these, members of the Royal Family are simply fallible human beings like the rest of us. Yet we still want to believe that some people are special. Perhaps we even need to believe it.

In the Middle Ages people were miraculously cured of terrible illnesses by touching the hem of the monarch's gown. In the twentieth century a visit from a member of the Royal Family can perform a similar miracle on a patient in hospital. Today we ascribe it to psychology, but whatever name it goes by the royal magic still exists.

No one has practised this magic more consistently or to greater effect than the Queen Mother. Octogenarian great grandmother she may be, like thousands of other women throughout Britain and the Commonwealth. But she is also very truly a Queen. When she walks into a room she brings with her an overwhelming sense that something very special is happening. When she leaves everyone feels better for having been in her presence.

The Queen Mum, as she is familiarly known, has the common touch in full measure. She is held in equal affection by all sections of society. What makes this so surprising is that she comes from an era when the daughters of Earls (her father was the fourteenth Earl of Strathmore) were brought up in a sheltered world with no expectation of having to cope with the stresses and strains of contact with the outside world.

Born with the century, a year before Edward VII came to the throne, she remains essentially what she always was; a wealthy and privileged Edwardian aristocrat. Her homes are run with a large retinue of servants and staff, and with all the efficiency and splendour of the great country houses before the First World War. Her speech retains the mannerisms of a bygone era, as anyone who overheard her refer to Patrick Lichfield as 'cousin fellow' as he took the wedding photographs of the Prince and Princess of Wales will have realised. She enjoys the leisurely lifestyle of women of her class. At Clarence House real afternoon tea is a ritual and luncheon parties are held every week. These hardly seem attributes to endear her to millions of people for whom life is a far greater struggle. Yet she has come to be known as Britain's favourite granny, and is held in higher esteem than any other member of the Royal Family, with the possible exception of her daughter, the Queen.

The reason lies in her great personal charm and strength of character. She has the rare gift of making the person she is talking to feel that no one else in the world matters. Her grandson Prince Charles, with whom she enjoys a close and companionable relationship, summed it up when he said, 'She belongs to that priceless brand of human beings whose greatest gift is to enhance the life of others.'

It is a gift that seems ideally suited to a family person, a wife and mother; and that was how the young Elizabeth Bowes Lyon expected her life to be when in 1923 she finally yielded to the persistent courtship of George V's son, the Duke of York, and agreed to marry him.

His rather harsh, strictly regimented upbringing had affected him physically and emotionally – he had a bad stammer and was inclined to depression and bursts of bad temper. Choosing Elizabeth as his wife was probably the best decision of his life, for her qualities were just what he needed to help rebuild his self-confidence. Her own relaxed attitude to his undoubtedly forbidding parents, George V and Queen Mary, helped him to feel more at ease with them himself. She encouraged him to see a therapist who helped him control his stammer. She accompanied him on formal and informal official duties, bringing to them her sense of fun and enthusiasm, gaining the title 'The Smiling Duchess' and changing people's view of her husband by her own popularity. She used her special gift to make her husband feel the most important person in the world, where before he carried with him the scars of a bleak childhood. Above all she created a warm, loving family home from which he gained a new strength of personality.

If it had not been for the Abdication of her brother-in-law, Edward VIII (the Duke of Windsor), and the accession of the Duke of York as George VI in 1936, that essentially domestic gift might never have been shared with so many millions. Although the Yorks had taken some share of royal duties they saw themselves as essentially private people. Bertie, as the Duke of York was known to his family, had received no training at all for the daunting task of being King. This, coupled with his acute shyness and stammer, made the prospect almost too awful to contemplate. When Edward VIII finally renounced the throne in order to marry Wallis Simpson there were many people in the country who felt that Bertie would not make the grade as King. They reckoned without the intensely held sense of duty which he inherited from Queen Mary. It was almost as though he had inherited the Duke of Windsor's share as well. Elizabeth, too, had been imbued with the belief that a privileged lifestyle like hers brought with it obligations which had to be fulfilled. 'Your work is the rent you pay for the room you occupy on earth', she is quoted as saying many years later. Then more than ever, Queen Elizabeth's ability to be supportive was essential to her husband. They met the challenge as an equal partnership.

In addition to the strong sense of duty they both shared, and to which people instinctively responded, the new Queen brought to the reign of George VI her own very special talent – the ability to make people feel loved, wanted and very special. It had helped her to create a happy family unit and since those momentous events in 1936 it has contributed to the sense of unity felt by all those who have an allegiance to the Crown, helping to create a sense of 'family' among the millions of disparate people who make up the United Kingdom and the Commonwealth.

The need to encourage a sense of unity and togetherness soon became essential as Britain faced the rigours of the second world war. George VI and Queen Elizabeth never considered leaving London, let alone going abroad, in order to find a safe refuge while the rest of the country bore the brunt of the bombing and the fighting. Their continued presence was a vital factor in maintaining morale. And when eventually peace returned it was clear from the King's worsened health that the stresses had been very hard to bear. His premature death at the age of fifty-six in 1952 deprived the country of a conscientious and hard-working monarch who had given himself heart and soul to his duty as he saw it. He had won over the hearts of the people, who came to value his sterling qualities above the glamour and glitter of the older brother who had abandoned the throne and his duty.

At this stage in her life Queen Elizabeth, who took the title Queen Mother at her own request, made it clear that she was ready to retire from public life. She bought the beautiful Castle of Mey, in the far north of her native Scotland, which she refurbished in her own opulent but homely style, and prepared for a widowhood devoted to her family, including two new grandchildren, Prince Charles and Princess Anne, and to creating a beautiful garden sheltered behind stone walls from the effects of the bleak Scottish climate.

She was probably the only one genuinely surprised to find that the public would not allow her to retreat from public engagements. Gradually, as she came to terms with her own personal grief, her sense of duty overcame her preference for a private lifestyle. One of her main concerns was to help her daughter, the new Queen Elizabeth II, to fulfil her own onerous responsibilities without being forced to neglect her own family life. While the Queen was on her six month extended Commonwealth tour in 1953 it was the Queen Mother who held the fort at home, giving Charles and Anne the security they might otherwise have missed with both parents away.

Since then the Queen Mother has consistently been one of the busiest members of the Royal Family. Her energy is phenomenal. She does not admit to illness but shows all the hardiness of her Scottish ancestors, using only homeopathic remedies if she feels unwell.

Like her own mother-in-law, Queen Mary, she has developed her own inimitable personal dress sense; pastel colours, floating fabrics, printed chiffons, large hats with upturned brims and spotted veils, glamorous beaded evening dresses and tiaras which make her look truly regal. Like Queen Mary her clothes are outside conventional fashion; they are a personal statement of her own unique personality. It is no secret that the Queen Mother intensely disliked her sister-in-law, the former Wallis Simpson. She blamed her for thrusting George VI into a life for which he was personally ill-suited and which placed a tremendous strain on his frail constitution. The fact that there was little love lost between the two women probably accounts for the apocryphal story that when Mrs Simpson was asked for her opinion of how the then Duchess of York could best help promote British fashion, the acid reply was, 'By staying at home!' Nevertheless it is the Queen Mother who developed a true personal style, while the Duchess of Windsor, as she later became, epitomised only the soulless chic of international fashion.

As with her dress, so with her way of life. The Queen Mother's energy and enthusiasm are clear from her many wide-ranging interests. She loves art, the theatre and ballet and she surrounds herself with theatrical people. Gardening is one of her passions. So too is horse-racing, an enthusiasm she shares with the Queen, although the Queen Mother's horses are steeplechasers, while the Queen specialises in flat racing. A long-time hobby has been salmon fishing, and she has taught her grandchildren and their partners to fish. For the Queen Mother old age has not meant a narrowing of her interests any more than it has meant a slowing down in her work. Paradoxically it seems that what keeps her young is not being over-protective of herself but keeping busy, active and informed.

A new royal ritual has developed over recent years. On the Queen Mother's birthday she emerges from Clarence House before a family lunch party to greet the crowds of well-wishers who gather to wish her a Happy Birthday. Young children bring flowers for her and she greets some of her keenest fans who appear year after year. Everyone is delighted to see her and to watch as she gives her famous little wave and broad smile. It is a simple ceremony but one which captures people's hearts year after year. The Queen Mother is genuinely loved because she is an unchanging landmark in a world where so much seems to have changed for the worse. She is true to herself. There is nothing phoney about her. She is sincere in her love for the public and they respond in their turn with a genuine and sincere love for her.

Michèle Brown

A GOLDEN CHILDHOOD

For those fortunate enough to be born into families of wealth and privilege, the Victorian and Edwardian eras seem to have offered a golden age of childhood. And by all accounts the early years of the Hon. Elizabeth Angela Marguerite Bowes Lyon, born on 4 August 1900 and just, therefore, qualifying as a Victorian, was an idyllic time.

Elizabeth was the youngest daughter and ninth child of Lord and Lady Glamis (later the Earl and Countess of Strathmore) whose family home was St Paul's Walden Bury, near Hitchin in Hertfordshire. As the youngest in so large a family, with brothers and sisters much older than herself, she might have suffered a lonely childhood. Fortunately, in 1902 a companion arrived in the nursery; her younger brother David. They grew up together almost like twins, playing in the woods and grounds at Bury and surrounded by pets, including Elizabeth's favourite, a Shetland pony called Bobs. There were also periods of residence at their London house, when they socialised with other little 'Honourables' like themselves and made friendships that were to last the rest of their lives.

Summer holidays were spent at the ancient family seat, Glamis Castle, reputed to be one of the most haunted castles in Scotland. Undaunted, young Elizabeth and David must have romped through corridors and rooms where the White Lady and, most famous of all, the Monster of Glamis were said to lurk. Lady Strathmore, their mother, did not believe in the old adage about children being seen and not heard, and in the evenings after dinner they joined in the songs around the piano and played parlour games with the guests. Time could hang heavily during these Scottish house parties unless everyone made an effort to have fun, and it was here that young Lady Elizabeth, as she became in 1904 when her father inherited the Earldom, developed her talent to amuse and entertain people – a talent for which, more than eighty years on, she is still famous.

Like most girls of her class at the time, Elizabeth did not go to school. Instead she and David were taught at home by a French governess and, later, by one from Germany. There were dancing classes and music lessons, and Elizabeth proved that she had inherited her mother's talent for playing the piano. She was also a member of the Girl Guides, through which she became a friend of Princess Mary, daughter of King George V.

Then on her birthday in 1914, as if to mark her transition from this tranquil upbringing to the worst realities of the adult world, war was declared between the United Kingdom and Germany. Almost overnight, things changed. Four of Elizabeth's brothers joined up and her sister, Lady Rose, went away for a speedy nursing training. Glamis Castle was converted to a convalescent home for wounded troops, and Elizabeth and her mother became involved in looking after the soldiers billeted in their splendid Dining Room. At a time when she might have been making her mark in Society, she was winding bandages and knitting socks and scarves for the troops of the local battalion. Then in 1915 came the news that the family had dreaded; Captain Fergus Bowes Lyon, the fourth-youngest brother, had been killed in action. Lady Elizabeth's golden childhood was over.

The inseparable pair, Elizabeth and her brother David, dressed for a dancing display in 1909.
David is wearing an outfit based on that worn by the family jester; the Strathmores were the last
family in Scotland to have their own private jester.

Preceding page: One of the earliest studies of Elizabeth Bowes Lyon, aged two,
in her high chair.

Lady Elizabeth at the age of seven. Around the time this photo was taken, she attended a charity fete and had her palm read by a gipsy. When her French governess asked what the gipsy had predicted, Elizabeth replied, 'She says I'm going to be a Queen when I grow up. Isn't it silly!'

With one of her first pet dogs in the grounds of Glamis Castle. The Queen Mother has always loved dogs, and they love her. While inspecting bomb damage in London during the war, she came across a woman who was trying to coax her dog out from under the rubble. 'Perhaps I might try,' suggested the Queen. 'I am rather good with dogs.'

In 1915 Lady Elizabeth is shown as a stall-holder at a wartime charity sale. Her cheerfulness made her very popular with the convalescing soldiers at Glamis – so much so that one man said that when he returned to the front he would wear a label reading, 'Please return to Glamis,' in case he was injured again.

THE DUCHESS OF YORK

Exactly when and where Elizabeth Bowes Lyon first met Albert, Duke of York, second son of George V, is something of a mystery. Elizabeth was a friend of Albert's sister, Princess Mary, and it may be that they met informally during a visit to Buckingham Palace. Other biographers have pinpointed their first meeting at a ball held in May 1920. Wherever, and whenever, they met, Elizabeth was by now an attractive and vivacious young woman, determined to make up for the opportunities she had lost during the war. Her social life was a busy one, but she was not a member of the cigarette-smoking, cocktail-drinking, sophisticated crowd who clustered around the Prince of Wales in the 1920s. She was approachable, amusing and easy to get along with, and having grown up surrounded by brothers and, more recently, convalescing soldiers, she was at ease in male company. Her favourite pastime was dancing and, according to those who knew her at that period, she was never short of admiring partners and would-be suitors.

It is hardly surprising that Prince Albert, four years older, was as captivated as all the others. Elizabeth was exactly the woman he needed; traditional but not stuffy, understanding but also fun. He arranged to visit Glamis on a number of occasions when Elizabeth was there, and was soon a regular guest of the family. Guessing her son's intentions, in the summer of 1921 Queen Mary also paid a visit to Glamis and was impressed by Lady Elizabeth's charm and confidence. King George approved of her too, but had his private doubts: 'You'll be a lucky fellow if she accepts you,' was his reaction when Bertie announced that he intended to propose.

There has been much speculation that Elizabeth twice turned down Bertie's offer of marriage. The Queen Mother has herself denied this, but other sources suggest that she was not easily persuaded to become a member of the Royal Family. Perhaps, after the strains of the war, she was simply not ready to accept the responsibilities that would fall on her as Duchess of York. Perhaps it took some time for her to fall in love with Bertie, whose chronic stammer and awkward manner were obvious drawbacks when it came to romance. What we do know for certain is that on 13 January 1923 Prince Albert went to stay for the weekend at St Paul's Walden Bury and that on the Saturday, during a walk in the gardens there, he proposed. Little guessing quite how dramatically it was to change her life, Lady Elizabeth said yes.

Preceding page: The Duke of York and his future Duchess: an official engagement photo. Lady Elizabeth gazes wistfully at the camera while Bertie looks understandably pleased with his prize. Among the wedding gifts they received during this engagement period were one thousand gold-eyed needles and two dozen pairs of wellington boots.

At 11.12 a.m. on 26 April 1923, Lady Elizabeth leaves her father's house in Bruton Street for Westminster Abbey. Plans to broadcast the ceremony over the radio had been dropped because the Archbishop of Canterbury feared that men might hear it in pubs, or that others would listen with their hats on.

A classic portrait, published in the *Illustrated London News* on 28 April 1923. On the Wednesday following the announcement of her engagement, Lady Elizabeth gave an interview to the members of the Press who had besieged her London home. King George and Queen Mary were so shocked when they were told about this that Elizabeth was instructed never to do it again. She heeded their opinion and to this day does not give personal interviews.

'We have all hoped, waited, so long for this romance to prosper, that we had begun to despair that she would ever accept him… He is the luckiest of men, and there's not a man in England today who doesn't envy him. The clubs are in gloom.'
CHIPS CHANNON.

The Wedding Group. Elizabeth, now Duchess of York, wears a lace train and veil lent by Queen Mary, but in a break with tradition her dress is decorated with machine-made Nottingham lace in an attempt to boost the flagging Nottingham lace industry.

Mother and Mother-in-Law.
Above: The Duchess of York arrives with her mother, the Countess of Strathmore, at the
British Empire Exhibition in April 1924. Behind the smiles there was tension, for Bertie had to
open the exhibition by making the first broadcast speech of his life. It was an agonizingly difficult
occasion. 'Bertie got through his speech all right, but there were some rather long pauses,'
wrote his father the following day.

Strolling in the grounds of Balmoral with Bertie and Queen Mary in 1924. Elizabeth got on well with everyone in her new family. Even King George, usually a stickler for punctuality, didn't seem to mind that she was always late. 'Elizabeth is with us now, perfectly charming, so well brought-up, a great addition to the family,' wrote Queen Mary.

The Duke and Duchess with their daughter Princess Elizabeth on 29 May 1926, the day on which she was christened. The baby Princess is wearing the traditional Honiton lace christening robe, originally made for Edward VII and used for every royal christening since then.

The Duchess of York in 1926. She and the Duke had been asked to undertake a tour to Australia and New Zealand, but doubts were cast on Bertie's ability to deliver the important speeches required during the visit. Elizabeth, determined that Bertie should not be humiliated by being left out, persuaded him to try one more speech therapist, a brilliant Australian called Lionel Logue. After a month's intensive treatment, during which he learned how to control his breathing, the Duke had improved so much that he set off on the tour with new-found confidence.

During a visit to France in 1931, the Queen Mother (then Duchess of York) went to see the Colonial Exhibition at Vincennes. It had been organised by the military leader Marshal Lyautey, who had virtually created modern Morocco for the French. He showed her round personally, but was depressingly formal and lacklustre until she turned to him and said, 'Monsieur le Marechal, you are such a powerful man. You created the beautiful country of Morocco and you have made this great exhibition. Would you do something for me?'
Surprised, the old man asked what he could do. 'The sun is in my eyes,' explained the Duchess. 'Could you make it disappear?' As she finished speaking, a cloud passed across the sun and it disappeared. Everyone looked up in amazement. 'Thank you,' she said. 'I knew you could do anything.' Marshal Lyautey, overcome by her charm, at last relaxed. 'I saw the cloud coming,' the Duchess quietly confessed to an onlooker.

Salmon fishing at Tokaanu in New Zealand, 1927. Despite the excellent fishing to be found in New Zealand, even a catch like this could not make up for the fact that the Duchess had to leave Princess Elizabeth behind in England for the five months of the tour.

27 June 1927. The Duke and Duchess, reunited with their daughter, received a rapturous welcome from their tour. In this picture from the Royal Archives at Windsor, they are shown greeting the crowds from the balcony of Buckingham Palace. Queen Mary, who had looked after the little Princess while her parents were away, protectively holds the umbrella while King George is obviously delighted. The tour had been recognised as a great success, and the Yorks' hard work and dedication to duty were widely admired. While their popularity blossomed, there was a growing sense of disapproval about the lifestyle of the Prince of Wales and his night-clubbing friends.

With her famous smile and charm, and her talent for putting people at their ease, the Duchess brought a new style to her royal duties. Above left: The Duchess enjoys a joke during a surprise visit to the Queen Alexandra Nursing Home for Wounded Soldiers, Putney Heath, in 1928. Above right: On a visit to the Middlesex Hospital in 1935 she meets young Jimmy Chart.

QUEEN ELIZABETH

For the next four years the Duke and Duchess of York settled down to enjoy family life with Princess Elizabeth and her sister, Princess Margaret Rose, born in August 1930 at Glamis. It was a happy time. In 1932 the King gave the Yorks the Royal Lodge at Windsor, and they set about restoring it and turning it into a proper country home. In 1933 the first corgi joined the royal household. In 1935 the nation celebrated King George's Silver Jubilee with fireworks and bonfires and processions. And there were, of course, balls and banquets, holidays in Scotland and occasional trips abroad to vary the routine. There were also some clouds looming on the horizon. The Depression threw thousands of people out of work. In Germany Adolf Hitler became Reich Chancellor. King George's health began to fail. And those who were concerned about the monarchy watched, with growing worry, the Prince of Wales's increasingly close relationship with Mrs Wallis Simpson, an American divorcee who had been presented at Court in 1931.

In 1936 the storm broke when, on 20 January, the King died at Sandringham and the Prince of Wales succeeded him as Edward VIII. It was a great loss for the Duke and Duchess of York, not just because they had been close to the King, but because his death seemed certain to bring to an end some of the old traditions of royalty – traditions which included a strong emphasis on duty and formality and high moral standards. The new King and his friends were not interested in formality, or, it seemed, in duty. When he was asked to open the Aberdeen Royal Infirmary in September 1936, Edward made an excuse for not going. The Duke and Duchess of York agreed to attend the ceremony in his place, and while they were doing their duty the King was spotted waiting for Mrs Simpson at Aberdeen Station. The story, and its implications, rapidly spread around the country, and so did the sense of unease.

In October that year Mrs Simpson was divorced from her second husband; in November, the King told the Prime Minister that he intended to marry her. The idea of a twice-divorced American Queen on the English throne was one which few people could contemplate, and when objections were made Edward talked seriously of abdication. From this point events took on a whirlwind quality. Spurred by sensational headlines, public opinion hardened against the King's

Preceding page: King George VI, Queen Elizabeth and the Princesses wearing their coronation crowns and robes. The coronation, on 12 May 1937, was the first to be broadcast and filmed for cinema newsreels.

marriage; the Duchess of York, concerned for her husband's happiness and perceiving Mrs Simpson as its main threat, erected a frosty barrier between them; meanwhile the King desperately sought a solution to the problem. There was none. The ultimatum was simple – give up Mrs Simpson or give up the Crown. By 8 December he had made his decision, and two days later he signed the instrument of Abdication. On 11 December 1936 the Duke of York was proclaimed King and Elizabeth became his Queen.

It was not a role that either of them took on enthusiastically. The stress of those final weeks was such that when the Duchess heard that she was to be Queen, she fell ill with flu. The new King, who chose to reign as George VI, told Lord Louis Mountbatten, 'I never wanted this to happen. I'm quite unprepared for it.'

June 1936: the lull before the storm. The Duke and Duchess (she still in black after the death of her father-in-law) and their daughters at *Y Bwthyn Bach,* a miniature Welsh thatched cottage presented to the little Princesses by the people of Wales in 1931 and erected at Royal Lodge, Windsor. Queen Mary insisted on inspecting it on her hands and knees and was impressed by the plumbing and the fully-equipped kitchen.

The King and Queen at a garden party during the State visit to France in 1938. Shortly before the visit was due to begin, the Queen's mother died. It looked as if she would have to dress in sombre black for the trip until Norman Hartnell, her designer, remembered that white was a colour of royal mourning. Within a fortnight her entire wardrobe had been remade. Paris was dazzled by such chic and the visit was an overwhelming success.

July 1939, the Blue Drawing Room, Buckingham Palace. On her return from Canada and the USA, Queen Elizabeth posed for Cecil Beaton wearing the gowns that had created such a sensation in Paris and Canada. By the time the pictures were published, war had been declared and Beaton was concerned that the grandeur and glamour of his portraits was inappropriate. He need not have worried. Grandeur and glamour were exactly what was needed during the first grey weeks of the war, and one of the photos of the Queen in her tiara was used on a Christmas card sent to every member of the armed forces, with the message, 'May God bless and protect you, Elizabeth R George RI.'

Throughout his life Cecil Beaton took many photos of the Queen Mother. After one particular sitting, when she had chosen the pictures she liked best, he suggested that some of the more obvious laughter lines could be concealed by careful retouching. The Queen Mother turned down the idea with the words, 'I would not want it to be thought that I had lived for all these years without having anything to show for it.'

The King and Queen with Mr and Mrs Roosevelt (far left) and Mr Roosevelt's mother (centre). With the threat of war hanging over Europe in 1939, the King decided to strengthen ties with Canada and the United States by going on tour. He received a rapturous welcome, the first King of England to set foot in America. There was an immediate friendship between the royal couple and their hosts and their parting was a sad one. Mrs Roosevelt recorded in her diary: 'As the train pulled out someone began singing "Auld Lang Syne"… and it seemed to me that there was something of our friendship and our sadness and something of the uncertainty of our futures in that song that I could not have said in any other words.'

THE WAR YEARS

After the triumph of the King and Queen's visit to Canada and America, and their even more triumphant return home, it seemed, just for a short time, as if the war might not materialise. But at the end of August the calm was broken by news of the Soviet-German Non-Aggression pact and on 3 September 1939 Neville Chamberlain announced that Britain was at war. The Princesses were at Balmoral at the time, and later went to live at Windsor Castle, which was considered to be the safest place for them. Queen Elizabeth meanwhile attended revolver practice on the lawns at Buckingham Palace and supervised the packing up of all the precious paintings and items of furniture. She also made time to read Hitler's *Mein Kampf,* which she despised.

Life at Buckingham Palace was far from comfortable. Food rations were strictly observed and when Eleanor Roosevelt came for a visit she was shocked by the turnip jam and egg powder that the Royal Family ate without complaint. On one occasion, during a trip to Lancashire, the Queen found that a lavish lunch had been laid on for her. 'We don't have any more food on the table at Buckingham Palace than is allowed to the ordinary householder according to the rations for the week,' she protested. 'In that case,' said the Mayor hosting the occasion, 'you'll be glad of a bit of a do like this.'

This kind of outward show of patriotism, and the very fact that the Royal Family refused to leave the country, were of immeasurable importance when it came to winning the war. And the Queen, carefully tracing a path through bombsites and talking sympathetically with those who had lost everything in the destruction, became a symbol of hope, 'a continuing inspiration to the Empire in the Fight against Nazi-ism', as one paper described her.

Preceding page: 'I'm glad we've been bombed. Now I can look the East End in the face,' the Queen told a policeman after Buckingham Palace had been hit. Here she and the King stand among the rubble after the bombing on 10 September 1940. This picture of them inspecting the damage was used on their Christmas card later that year.

October 1939, the Blue Drawing Room, Buckingham Palace. Only months after Cecil Beaton had photographed her in this room, the Queen is pictured there again, this time leading a working party of women from the royal household in making clothes and surgical dressings for the Red Cross.

South London, November 1940. The King and Queen visit children in their bunks at a deep shelter in South London. Visits like these affected her deeply. 'The destruction is so awful and the people so wonderful – they deserve a better world,' she wrote in a letter to Queen Mary.

On a visit to an agricultural camp in 1944, the King and Queen talk to female volunteers hoeing a mangold field. Despite the fact that this kind of visit was a terrific morale-booster for everyone who met them, the King was frustrated at not being able to do anything more positive. In an effort to make up for the fact that he could not go and fight, he spent two evenings a week making parts for RAF guns.

Opposite: The King and Queen spent the weekends with their daughters at Windsor. Here Queen Elizabeth poses with the Princesses in July 1941.
Above: A family gathering around the piano at Royal Lodge, Windsor, in April 1942.
When it was suggested that her daughters be sent to Canada for safety, the Queen is reported to have said, 'The Princesses will never leave without me, I will not leave without the King – and the King will never leave.' With those words the Royal Family became a symbol of Britain's determination to stick the war out, and pictures like these reassured millions.

'She belongs to that priceless brand of human beings whose greatest gift is to enhance the life of others.'
PRINCE CHARLES.

The Queen with her sister-in-law, Princess Marina, the Duchess of Kent, at Windsor in 1944, two years after the death of the Duke of Kent in an air crash. The Kents had been friends of the Prince of Wales and Mrs Simpson, and the Abdication crisis had created a certain tension between them and the Yorks.

V.E. Day, 8 May 1945. The King and Queen, the Princesses and Winston Churchill greet the quarter of a million people celebrating victory outside Buckingham Palace. That night Princess Elizabeth and Princess Margaret were allowed to join the revellers for half an hour, and cheered their parents from the Mall.

At a Buckingham Palace Garden Party given in June 1945 for repatriated prisoners of war, the Queen talks to soldiers and airmen.

INTERLUDE

Whatever their fears during the Abdication crisis in 1936, King George VI and Queen Elizabeth had between them succeeded in raising the popularity of the Crown to a level almost unknown since the time of Queen Victoria. Any doubts that had been expressed about their ability when they were so suddenly pushed into the limelight, had been overcome by the dedicated example they had set during the war. And there was particular recognition for the role Queen Elizabeth had played – not just in the war, but in the making of the King. As one contemporary commentator described her, she was, 'A woman who new that change was coming and went with the tide. The woman who knew, when she married "Bertie", that a wife could make or mar him. The woman who had made "Bertie"'. With her help, he had conquered his speech impediment. With her at his side he had brought his country to victory in a just war. Thanks to her guiding hand, and her emphasis on duty and patriotism, in Princess Elizabeth the country had the ideal heir to the throne.

The years after the war were a time for the King and Queen to enjoy the peace and popularity they had worked so hard for.

Preceding page: An official photograph of the King and Queen at home in their private apartment at Buckingham Palace, taken to celebrate their Silver Jubilee on 26 April 1948.

In 1947 the Royal Family toured South Africa, the first time that the King and Queen and their daughters had gone on tour together. They are seen here in Durban, watching a march-past. Princess Elizabeth had become unofficially engaged to Prince Philip of Greece the previous August, but the news was not announced until their return from tour.

During the South African tour, the train on which the Royal Family travelled made a stop at Swellendam, an Afrikaner town where Nationalist feelings were running high. As the Queen waved to the crowd gathered on the platform, one old Afrikaner told her that although he was pleased to see the Royal Family, he didn't like being governed by Westminster. The Queen nodded sympathetically and, referring to her ancestry said, 'I understand perfectly. We feel the same in Scotland.'

A group photograph taken after the wedding of Princess Elizabeth and the Duke of Edinburgh on 20 November 1947. As rationing was still in force, the Princess was allowed one hundred extra clothing coupons for her trousseau. The King was sad to lose his daughter: 'I am so proud of you & thrilled at having you so close to me on our long walk in Westminster Abbey,' he wrote to her, 'but when I handed your hand to the Archbishop I felt I had lost something very precious.'

Above: Queen Elizabeth attends a Gala Performance at Covent Garden in July 1951.

Opposite: The King and Queen attend the Service of the Order of the Garter in St George's Chapel, Windsor in 1950. The strain of nearly two years of ill health, during which, at one point, it was feared his right leg might have to be amputated, shows on the King's face.

The King and Queen with their grandchildren, Prince Charles and Princess Anne, in a photo taken to celebrate Prince Charles's third birthday on 14 November 1951. Queen Elizabeth's smile hides her worries about the King, who, it had been diagnosed, was suffering from lung cancer.

On 6 February 1952 King George died in his sleep at Sandringham. Ten days later Queen Elizabeth, now the Queen Mother, is photographed as her carriage follows the King's funeral procession on its slow journey to St George's Chapel, Windsor. The King's death came as a great blow to many. It was not until he had died that his qualities of quiet perseverence, honour and duty were fully recognised. Too late, the nation realised that it had lost the monarch it loved.

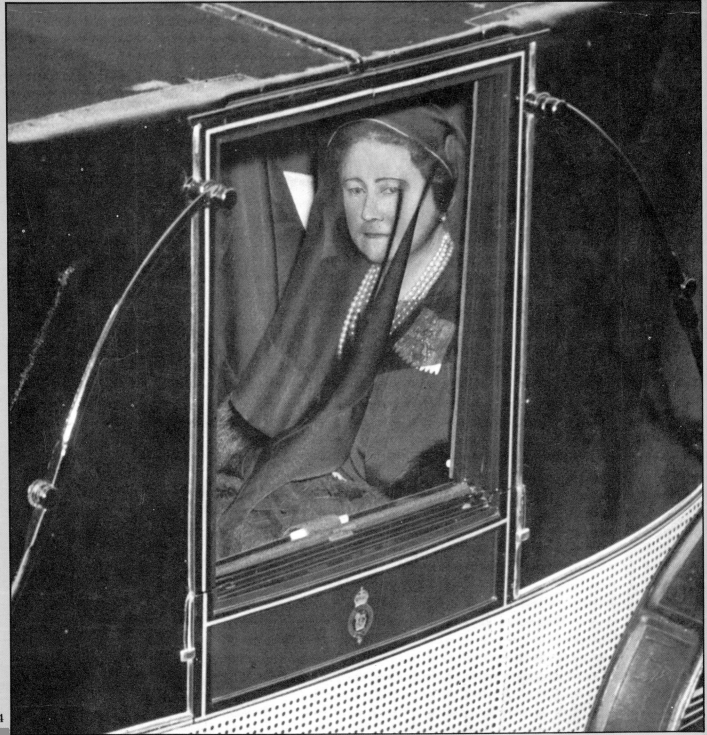

A NEW LIFE

Queen Elizabeth has now been Queen Mother for more years than she was Queen consort. With the passing of those years we have become so familiar with her role as mainstay of the Royal Family that we tend to forget it is a job she herself created. Other royal widows have gone into seclusion, like Queen Victoria, or become formidable dowagers, like Queen Mary. The Queen Mother's greatest triumph has been the fact that she has so successfully created a new life and a new role for herself.

Preceding page: Grandmother Alone. With Prince Charles and Princess Anne at Royal Lodge, Windsor in April 1954.

Her Majesty's Pleasure. From her earliest years the Queen Mother has loved dancing. Here, she joins in the Dashing White Sergeant at the Royal Caledonian Ball, in 1959.

Royal Champion. The Queen Mother's passion for horse racing and her success as a breeder and owner are almost legendary. At her London residence, Clarence House, she listens to the racing results as they are broadcast from the specially installed bookies' 'blower'. This picture from the television film *Royal Champion* shows her with ex-jockey Terry Biddlecombe.

Farmer. At a cattle show on the Black Isle, Ross-shire, the Queen Mother comes face to face with a prize bull. As the owner of a herd of Aberdeen Angus she is something of a cattle expert, and when she is staying at the Castle of Mey, her private home in the north of Scotland, she often visits local agricultural shows.

Beachcomber. Visitors to the north Norfolk coast are sometimes surprised to see the unmistakable figure of the Queen Mother exercising her corgis on the beach. Here, she is accompanied by the Duchess of Grafton.

Above: Casual Charm. Wherever she goes, and even when she is relaxing, the Queen Mother cannot resist some discreet public relations work. While the Queen, wearing pink, concentrates on the horses at the Badminton Horse Trials, the Queen Mother enjoys an amusing chat with the crowd of onlookers.

Opposite: Countrywoman. Nearly forty years after her first fishing trip to New Zealand, the Queen Mother is pictured there again, this time fishing at Lake Wanaka in 1966. Only in the last year or two has she been persuaded to fish from the bank, rather than wading out into the water.

Churchwoman. A delightful picture of the Queen Mother with the clergy and choir of All Saints Church, Ascot. Like all her family, she is a member of the Church of England and a regular church-goer. She is also a supporter of the ecumenical movement which aims to unite all Christian churches. In 1959 she and Princess Margaret went to the Vatican for an audience with the Pope, and in Scotland she attends services of the Church of Scotland. This concern for the broad spectrum of religion has influenced at least one of her grandchildren, Prince Charles.

The Royal Professional. No other member of the Royal Family can rival the Queen Mother for the sheer professionalism and energy she brings to everything she does. A skilled public performer, she understands the importance of communicating with her people – and this she does with unique charm and a sense of humour that makes her a favourite with photographers and film crews. Opposite: Posing with a pint on an official visit to a pub. Above: Standing in the snow with the crew who made *Royal Champion*, a television programme about her horses. The Queen Mother is totally at ease in front of television cameras; her only dislike when it comes to filming is the intrusiveness of the sound boom.

On duty. At a time of life when most other people are content to retire and watch the world go by, the Queen Mother continues to fulfil more than a hundred official functions each year. Her stamina is legendary; sometimes she fits five or six engagements into a single day in a punishing schedule that would exhaust her grandchildren. Above left: At the Festival of Remembrance held in the Royal Albert Hall. The Queen Mother's favourite colours are pastels, particularly shades of blue and lavender, and she is rarely seen in black. Above right: Inspecting the Pensioners at the Royal Hospital, Chelsea on Founder's Day.
Opposite: Each year the Queen Mother presents bunches of shamrock to the Irish Guards, and their Irish wolfhound mascot, on the St Patrick's Day Parade. Being a dog-lover, she also makes a practice of offering the mascot a sweet or two.

Eighty Years On. There were many celebrations to mark the Queen Mother's 80th birthday, but none was as moving as the special Birthday Thanksgiving Service, opposite, held at St Paul's Cathedral on 15 July 1980. Prayers were said by representatives of the Catholic Church and the Church of Scotland, as well as by the Archbishop of Canterbury, Dr Runcie, who later declared that it was the most beautiful service he had conducted.

Birthday Honours. 1980 also saw the start of a new tradition. On the morning of her birthday, 4 August, the Queen Mother emerged from the gates of Clarence House, her London home, to greet the thousands of well-wishers waiting outside.
Above right: 1987: Flowers from a new generation of admirers.
Above left: An informal birthday portrait, with one of her corgis. The first royal corgi, Dookie, joined the family in 1933, at the request of Princess Elizabeth. The Queen Mother was obviously not deterred by Dookie's ferocity, for she has been faithful to the breed ever since.

Of all the photos taken to celebrate her birthday, none was as delightful as this classic portrait of the Queen Mother with her daughters. It was taken by Norman Parkinson, who dressed all three in matching blue satin capes for the occasion. According to Princess Margaret, the photo session was a happy occasion and they laughed and joked their way through it.

'Your work is the rent you pay for the room you occupy on earth.'
THE QUEEN MOTHER

A Taste for Travel.
By old-fashioned ship or new-fangled helicopter, on official visits or private trips, the Queen Mother loves to travel – and widowhood has not slowed her down. The list of countries she has visited seems almost endless, and her enthusiasm for adding to it is unlimited. In 1984 she made a visit to Venice and enjoyed her first ride in a gondola.

The End of an Era – A New Generation.
Above: 29 April 1986. It has been widely reported that the Queen Mother believed the strain of the Abdication and the stress of becoming Sovereign contributed to her husband's premature death. She certainly never achieved a full reconciliation with the Duke and Duchess of Windsor before the Duke's death in 1972. Now, as the coffin bearing the Duchess is carried from St George's Chapel, Windsor, one of the most painful chapters of the Queen Mother's life comes to a close.

Above: The Queen Mother, accompanied by the new generation of royal princesses, in pensive mood on Remembrance Day 1987. With her are the Duchess of York (a title that the Queen Mother herself once held), the Princess Royal and the Princess of Wales. Both the Princess of Wales and the Duchess of York stayed with the Queen Mother for a few weeks at the beginning of their engagements, learning from her some of the essence of royalty and preparing for their transformation from commoner to princess – a transformation which, more than sixty years ago, the Queen Mother experienced first-hand.

A kiss for Zara and Peter Phillips, the Princess Royal's two children, as they come ashore from the royal yacht *Britannia*.

With Prince Charles at Scrabster, August 1986. Prince Charles is said to be the Queen Mother's favourite grandchild and he shares her interest in art and gardening.

Great-grandmother. Prince William, first child of the Prince and Princess of Wales and second in line to the throne, was christened on 4 August 1982 – his great-grandmother's eighty-second birthday.

Opposite: Matriach. Mother and Daughter.

At Ascot 1986, the Queen Mother and the Princess of Wales share a joke. The Queen Mother knows what it is to be constantly in the public eye, and her understanding and advice has helped the Princess to cope with the stress of her phenomenal popularity.

Royal Magic – the admiring looks say it all.

The Queen Mother.
Wife of one sovereign, mother of another, symbol of courage throughout the war years, public relations executive *par excellence,* horse-breeder, gardening expert, dog-lover, founder and mainstay of the modern royal family – the Queen Mother is all of these. But above all she is a radiant and graceful Queen, and her story is an inspiration to us all.

The Queen Mother at eighty-seven, photographed with her corgi, Ranger, at Clarence House.

'Ever since I remember my grandmother has been the most wonderful example of fun, laughter, warmth, infinite security and, above all else, exquisite taste in so many things.'
PRINCE CHARLES

Picture Acknowledgements

Cover: Lionel Cherraualt

BBC Hulton Picture Library 15, 18, 24, 26, 36 left, 40, 41, 47, 48, 50, 51, 58-9, 61, 65, 80, 94; Cecil Beaton, Camera Press, London 42; Lionel Cherraualt 78 left, 81 left, 89, 92; Anwar Hussein 84; The Illustrated London News Picture Library 22; The Keystone Collection 37, 57; The National Portrait Gallery 16; Robin Nunn 88; Norman Parkinson, Camera Press, London 82; Popperfoto 13, 17, 19, 30, 32, 49, 53, 54, 55, 60, 62, 64, 67, 72, 86; Copyright reserved. Reproduced by gracious permission of Her Majesty The Queen 25, 27, 28, 34, 36 right, 44, 45, 52; Rex Features 70-1, 73, 74-5, 76, 78 right, 87, 91; 'Royal Champion' – Central Independent Television plc 68, 77; Snowdon, Camera Press, London 95; Syndication International, London 2, 69, 79, 81 right, 90.